Castaway

David Macphail

Illustrated by **David Atkinson**
and **Judy Stevens**

OXFORD
UNIVERSITY PRESS

Contents

Foreword	4

I. THE OUTWARD JOURNEY, 1703 — 6

Selkirk's Early Life	6
The Expedition Begins	6
Privateers	8
War of the Spanish Succession	9
Life at Sea	10
Navigation	12
The *Cinque Ports*	14
Captain Dampier and the Prize	15
Round the Cape	16
Trouble Brewing	17
Seaworthy?	19

II. CASTAWAY — 21

Juan Fernández Island	24
Stradling's Fate	30
Dampier's Fate	31
The *Duke* and *Dutchess*	35

III. THE JOURNEY HOME, 1709 — 40

Aboard	40
Back to a Life at Sea	43
Home	47
The Real Robinson Crusoe	51
Castaway	52
Note on Sources	53
Glossary	54
Index	55

Foreword

A wild, hairy man dressed in goatskins ...

In 1709 two English ships, the *Duke* and the *Dutchess*,[1] approached the remote island of Juan Fernández in the South Pacific. Few Englishmen had ever visited this strange, exotic place which lay hundreds of kilometres to the west of Chile, far away from any trade routes. As the ships skirted the coast, the sailors gazed up in awe at the island's wild and rugged landscape: its steep sea-cliffs, its jagged volcanic mountains overhung with clouds, and its rich, fertile valleys.

The two ships had recently rounded Cape Horn. The men aboard were starving and sick, and in dire need of fresh water and supplies. They anchored near a wide bay, then sent a landing party ashore to investigate.

The landing party of eight men were stunned to see a man appearing at the edge of the trees. At least, he looked like a man. A wild, hairy man, dressed in goatskins and waving a white cloth on a stick. For a moment they wondered if he was even human. They demanded he speak, but he struggled to do so, as he'd forgotten how. The man raised his arms and blurted out his first word in many years:

'Marooned.'

[1] This is an old-fashioned spelling of the word 'duchess'.

This man was Alexander Selkirk, a Scotsman. They soon discovered that he'd been living on the island alone for the last four and a half years, having been marooned by another ship.

This book is based on an actual interview between Selkirk and a journalist, Richard Steele, which took place at the end of 1711. Steele was amazed by Selkirk's story.

WHO'S WHO

Richard Steele
journalist

Richard Steele's interview notes
1711

Today, I learned first-hand of the hardships which were endured by Alexander Selkirk during his time on Juan Fernández Island. I carried out an interview for my journal *The Englishman* in a coffee house in Bury Street, London.

As I shook the hand of the man I had heard so much about, and looked into his eyes, it seemed to me that he had long been separated from company. He paid no heed to the ordinary things going on around him. It was as if he was sunk in thought, and yet, there was a strong and cheerful seriousness in his look.

A man of good sense, he gave me an account of his life, and the four and a half years he spent as a **castaway** on the remote island of Juan Fernández.

Selkirk became a celebrity thanks to Steele and two popular books in which he featured. Both these books told the remarkable true-life story of how Selkirk was discovered living completely alone on a remote island in the South Pacific.

Selkirk's tale captured the imagination of the world, and it also gave birth to a legend. At its heart, it is the tale of a man who found peace in loneliness, and who returned home only to lose it again.

imagine!

Can you imagine what it would be like to be stranded on a deserted island for four years? How would you survive? And what would life as a castaway be like?

I. THE OUTWARD JOURNEY, 1703

Selkirk's Early Life

Alexander Selkirk was born in 1680 in the harbour village of Largo in Fife, Scotland, the youngest son of John and Euphan Selkirk. John was a tanner and shoemaker.

Alexander was a rough, quarrelsome boy with a foul temper, at odds with his brothers and the world in general. His father once warned him that his violent behaviour would lead him to a bad end. Young Alexander failed to take heed, however, and in 1695, at the age of 15, he was in trouble and called to appear before a hearing of village **elders**. The boy didn't hang around for the hearing. He ran off to sea before it took place.

The Expedition Begins

By 1703 Selkirk had already been away from home for eight years and was an experienced seaman and navigator. September of that year found him employed as **ship's master** on a vessel called the *Cinque Ports*, commanded by Captain Charles Pickering. On 11th September, the ship left the port of Kinsale in Ireland, along with its sister ship, the *St George*.

Safety in numbers

Ships in the 1700s often travelled in consort (in pairs). This was mainly for protection against pirates and foreign ships.

WHO'S WHO
Alexander Selkirk
ship's master for *Cinque Ports*

WHO'S WHO
Captain Charles Pickering
captain of *Cinque Ports*

WHO'S WHO
William Dampier
captain of *St George* (sister ship of *Cinque Ports*) and leader of the expedition

The ships were headed on a long and arduous voyage around the tip of South America. They carried a 'letter of marque' from the Lord High Admiral of England. This was a licence to attack England's enemies, capture their ships and bring any plunder home. Ships like Pickering's and Dampier's, and their crews, were called 'privateers'.

Expedition plan

- Kinsale, Ireland
- SOUTH AMERICA
- destination: South Pacific Ocean
- Juan Fernández
- Cape Horn

Privateers

Being a privateer was rather like being a pirate, but with a key difference. Privateers were in the service of the monarch and, unlike pirates, privateer captains were greatly respected – even though they attacked ships and stole treasure. Many private investors put their money into privateering, paying to fit out ships and hire crews. This was a business which would make some of them very rich.

Privateers preferred easy targets, such as small ships travelling alone. However, if the crew were desperate enough and the prize great enough, they would often go for bigger prey.

The Cinque Port's *letter of marque*

The privateer code

Keeping order on the ship was incredibly important. Before they left port, each man signed a written document called the Articles of Agreement. This was a kind of privateer's code: a set of rules that everyone had to follow. It established how large a share of the **booty** each man would get, how feuds would be settled and how any offences on board would be punished. It was sometimes written into the agreement that no man was to be marooned as a punishment; many sailors feared being abandoned on a deserted shore.

War of the Spanish Succession

Europe was at war between 1701 and 1714. The War of the Spanish Succession pitted England, Austria and Holland against Spain and France. The war was fought over who would take over the vacant throne of Spain, and England used every means it could to impede the Spanish war effort. Using privateers to attack Spanish and French ships was one of those means.

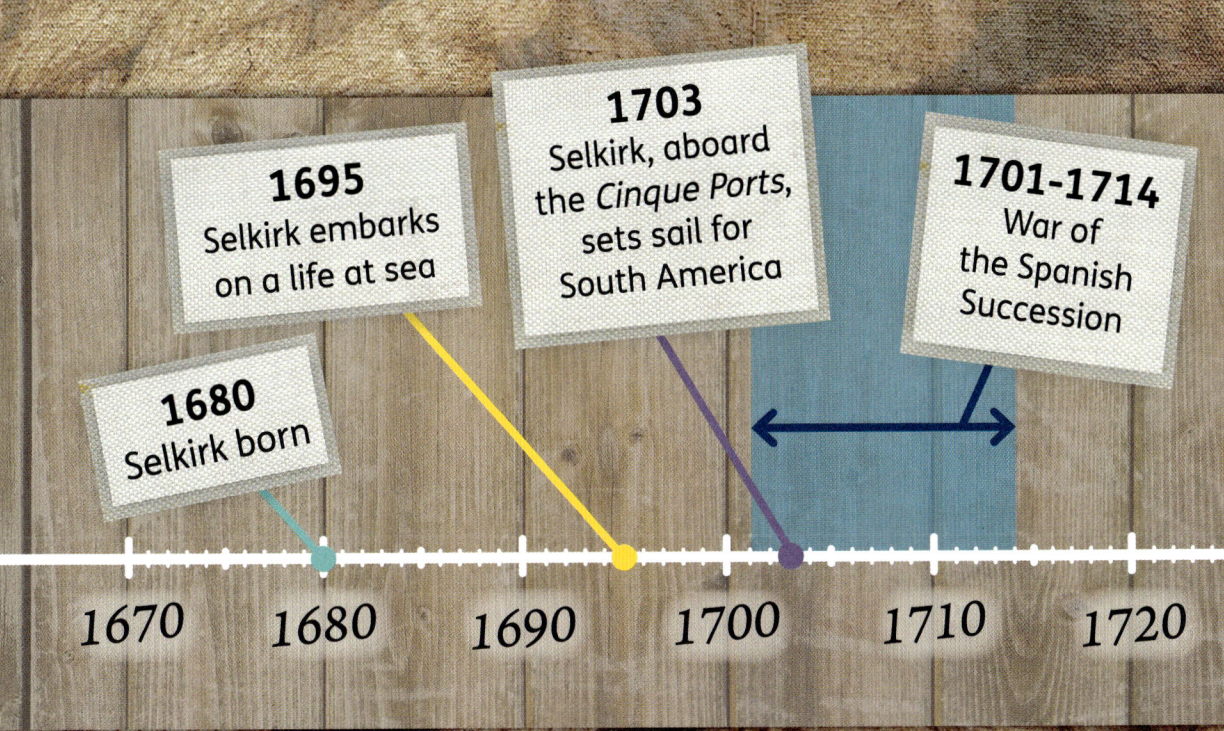

1680 Selkirk born

1695 Selkirk embarks on a life at sea

1703 Selkirk, aboard the *Cinque Ports*, sets sail for South America

1701-1714 War of the Spanish Succession

Spain controlled most of South America and the South Pacific, including its ports. This made sailing from England to South America extremely hazardous; the only safe places for an English ship to stop were uninhabited islands or places the Spanish had not yet claimed.

Life at Sea

Life at sea often involved long periods of boredom, broken by short, sharp bursts of action. Lots of young, feisty sailors locked away together in close confinement often led to conflict and discipline was always a problem.

imagine! What would it be like to be at sea for months – away from home, family and friends?

When they weren't working, the crew spent most of their lives below deck with the guns. Here they ate their meals, and here they slept, in hammocks hung from beams. There was very little natural light in the bowels of the ship. After living in such cramped, stuffy conditions for weeks – let alone months – the stench of the unwashed men would have been foul.

Food supplies on board ships had to be preserved for months or even years. Supplies would include:

- Ship's biscuits (or 'tooth breakers'): the staple of the crew's diet. Cheap and long-lasting, they were made using little other than flour and water.
- Beef, salted and packed in barrels: could remain preserved for up to two years.
- Flour, suet, raisins, vinegar, cheese (hard and tasteless) and dried cod. Also packed in barrels.

Quite often, when the ship's cook opened the barrels they would find that the food had spoiled, or it would be writhing with **weevils**.

On long voyages, ships often called at trading ports to restock their supplies and give the men a rest. Locals would sail up to the ships in small boats, clamouring to trade and barter.

However, in hostile waters, the privateers acted differently; they simply took what they needed without asking.

The life of a privateer was perilous. If captured by the enemy, they could expect to be hanged, or imprisoned, or sent to work as a slave in a Spanish silver mine. Yet the men endured it because of the lure of great riches.

Privateer life

Pros:
- adventure
- travel
- treasure!

Cons:
- peril
- poor food
- stinky sleeping deck!

Navigation

As ship's master, Selkirk's main job was to navigate the seas. Navigation was immensely difficult. Nautical charts (like maps) were not very reliable and working out a ship's position at sea was problematic, even in familiar waters. Piloting a ship across the Atlantic Ocean, around stormy Cape Horn at the southern point of South America and into the virtually unknown South Seas would have been an enormous task.

Navigating the oceans in those days was all about measuring angles: the angle between the horizon and a celestial body (the planets, the sun or other stars); or a vertical line and a celestial body; or even between one celestial body and another. Any good navigator worth his salt could pinpoint a ship's 'latitude' (how far north or south a ship was from the equator).

Using a backstaff to measure how high the sun is

Selkirk possessed his own navigational tools that could help him do this.

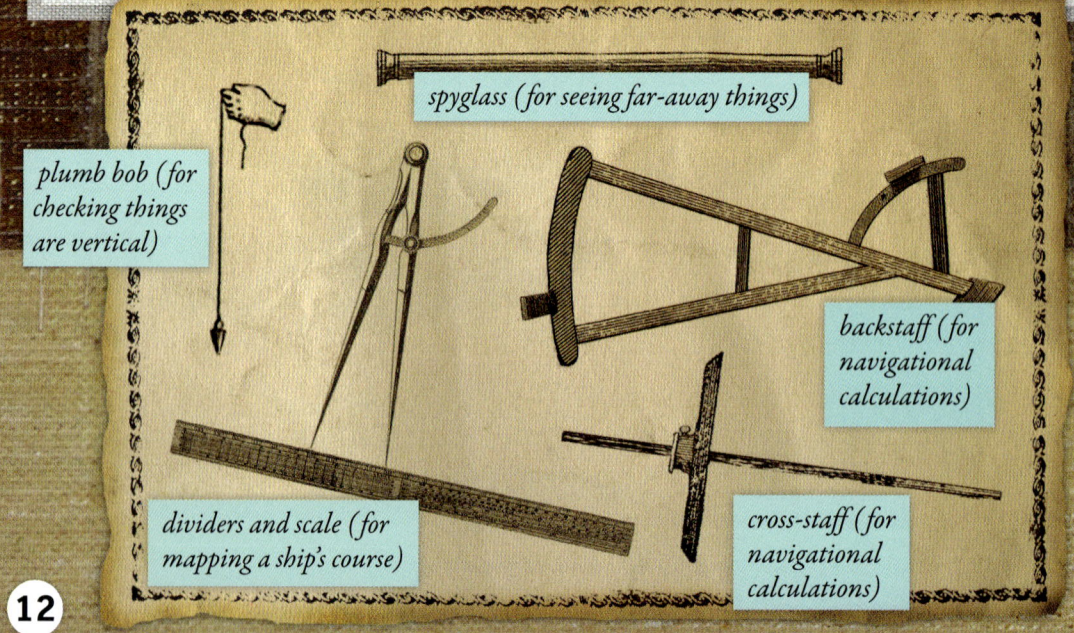

spyglass (for seeing far-away things)

plumb bob (for checking things are vertical)

backstaff (for navigational calculations)

dividers and scale (for mapping a ship's course)

cross-staff (for navigational calculations)

sundial (for checking the time during the day)

nocturnal (for checking the time at night)

ship's charts

Yet even with all these tools, there was no reliable way to work out a ship's 'longitude' (how far a ship was east or west). Quite often it came down to 'dead reckoning', which involved calculating a ship's position based on where it was yesterday and how far it was thought to have travelled. The problem with using dead reckoning was that it was easy to get it wrong, which would mean that every position estimated after the mistake would be wrong too. The more mistakes a navigator made, the more lost they became.

lines of latitude

lines of longitude

The *Cinque Ports*

Selkirk's ship, *Cinque Ports*, was quite small at 130 tonnes.[2] It carried 20 cannons and 90 men. Privateer ships were always overcrowded when they set out, as they needed the extra men to crew any enemy ships they captured. There were often only one or two experienced mariners aboard and, on the outward journey, Selkirk was one of them.

Most of the crew was made up of the most disadvantaged members of society: the poor, the dispossessed, debtors and ex-convicts. For these people the voyage offered them a second chance, a life of adventure and possible riches.

The *Cinque Ports* was equipped with about nine months of supplies and a range of **munitions**.

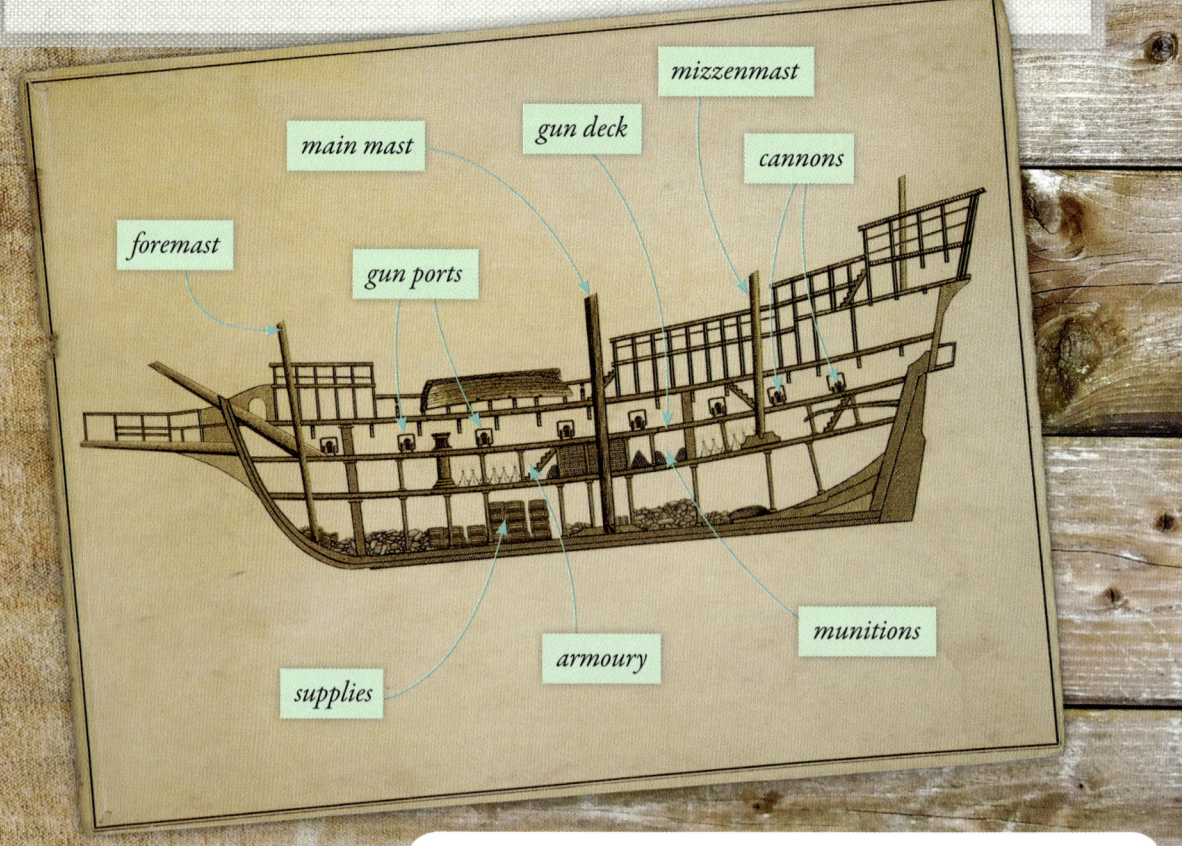

[2] This means that the ship could carry cargo of the same weight as 130 'tuns' – wooden casks for transporting liquid.

Captain Dampier and the Prize

You had to be a particular kind of person to want to go to sea as a career privateer. William Dampier, captain of the *Duke*, was a prime example: a true adventurer. A hardened, daring man with dark eyes, he voyaged around the globe several times and, in 1688, had become the first Englishman to explore Australia. He'd endured hurricanes, sea-battles, **mutinies** and forced marches. Dampier was every bit the fearless buccaneer who loved the sea as much as he loved gold, and knew the South Seas better than any living Englishman. He wrote books about his adventures, which became very popular.

Captain Dampier
Personal achievements

- First Englishman to explore Australia
- Experienced adventurer, navigator and pirate raider
- Circumnavigated the globe three times
- Wrote a best-selling book called *A New Voyage Round the World* based on his adventures

The scheme to attack the Spanish and French in the South Seas was Dampier's idea. His plan was to sail around Cape Horn, seize enemy ships and raid coastal towns. More than anything, Dampier's eye was on the biggest prize of all, the Manila **galleon**.

The great prize

The Manila galleon was a Spanish treasure ship that set out from Manila in the Philippines for Acapulco in Mexico in June of each year. It carried goods to the value of millions of Spanish dollars (known by pirates as 'pieces of eight') as well as gold, silver, jewels and many other precious items. The galleons the Spanish used to make this trip were the largest and richest trading vessels in the world and an English ship had only captured one once, back in 1587.

Round the Cape

It was a long and difficult voyage. Fever struck and many died – the crew of the *Cinque Ports* fell in number from 90 to 42. Their captain, Charles Pickering, was one of those who died. He was replaced by a **lieutenant** called Thomas Stradling, a less experienced seaman, aged around 21 and from a wealthy family.

Thomas Stradling
new captain of *Cinque Ports*

It soon became clear to all on board that Selkirk did not get on with the new captain and they argued frequently about how best to run the ship.

In January 1704, the *Cinque Ports* and the *St George* rounded Cape Horn. They had been at sea for five months. The food was rotting, the ship was in disrepair and many sailors were suffering from scurvy. The crew were hungry, exhausted and, worst of all, they had nothing to show for it all.

Scurvy

Disease killed more sailors than anything else. The most common disease was scurvy, which was caused by lack of vitamin C (found in fresh fruit and vegetables). The symptoms ranged from bleeding gums and sore joints right up to fever and death. Sailors called it 'the scourge of the sea'.

Juice from citrus fruits would have cured the crew's scurvy.

Trouble Brewing

In an act of desperation, the *St George* and the *Cinque Ports* attacked a large, well-armed French merchant ship. The battle lasted seven hours, but the privateers were outfought. Nine men were killed and many injured. Dampier ordered them to break off the pursuit, much to the crew's disgust.

Later, they raided the coastal town of Santa Maria. This failed miserably when the raiding party was ambushed by Spanish troops.

Then their luck changed a little, as they came upon a Spanish merchant ship called the *Asunción*. They surprised its crew and captured the ship easily.

Asunción booty
- flour
- other food and drink
- bales of wool and linen

Vessels that were captured by privateers were called 'prize ships' and privateers often added them to their fleet. Selkirk was put in charge of the *Asunción* and the mood of the crew was restored until Dampier suddenly gave orders to abandon the *Asunción* – for no good reason, as far as the crew were concerned.

The crew of both ships were outraged. They accused Dampier of throwing away their hopes of getting rich, and of pilfering the best of the ship's cargo for himself. After this incident, the two captains Dampier and Stradling fell out.

imagine! How do you think the crew of the *Asunción* felt when they were captured by the *St George* and the *Cinque Ports*?

Captain Dampier took the *St George* off for the coast of Peru in search of the Manila galleon, leaving the *Cinque Ports* to carry on alone.

Asunción captured

Asunción set adrift – ships part ways

journey of the St George

journey of the Cinque Ports

The crew aboard the *Cinque Ports* became hostile towards Captain Stradling. Selkirk was one of the ringleaders and, fearing mutiny, Stradling had Selkirk locked in a storeroom for a short time.

Cinque Ports ship's log

17th August 1704, South Pacific
Please note ship's master Mr Selkirk has been disciplined for his misdemeanour.

In September 1704, the *Cinque Ports* arrived at Juan Fernández – a small, uninhabited island in the South Pacific. The crew were relieved, for the **hull** of the *Cinque Ports* was leaking and the crew had to pump out water day and night to keep the ship from sinking. Their supplies, too, were almost at an end.

Seaworthy?

Selkirk was convinced that the ship was unseaworthy. He explained that **shipworms** had bored into the oak timbers and the hull would soon give way. It would never survive a long ocean voyage. He wanted to 'careen' the ship.

Careening a ship

1 ship is dragged ashore and turned on its side

2 hull is treated to kill off worms

3 damaged timbers can be replaced

Stradling didn't agree with Selkirk that the ship should be careened. Such repairs would take days. He reminded Selkirk that they were in hostile waters – a Spanish **man-of-war** might appear at any time, so this island was no place to linger. Besides, the crew were **mutinous**. They needed a prize.

Selkirk flew into a rage, accusing Stradling of putting everyone's lives at risk. He yelled that he would rather stay on the island than sail on an unseaworthy vessel with a bad commander like Stradling. He appealed to the rest of the crew to stand with him, but none did. They wanted to leave the island too. Stradling saw an opportunity to get rid of his troublesome ship's master then and there. He called Selkirk's bluff. He gave orders for Selkirk to be dumped on the beach.

Selkirk ranted and raved as Stradling and a few others rowed him ashore and then shoved him off the boat. Only now, as the oarsmen heaved his **sea chest** on to the beach, along with a few supplies, did he realize what was about to happen. He was to be marooned.

As the boat pushed off, Selkirk waded into the water up to his knees, pleading: 'Please, I have changed my mind. Take me back!' But the *Cinque Ports* sailed away.

imagine!

How do you think Selkirk felt as he watched the *Cinque Ports* disappear over the horizon? How might he have felt about the argument with Stradling?

II. CASTAWAY

An account based on Richard Steele's interview with Alexander Selkirk

I was sure they would come back for me, even as I watched the ship disappear over the horizon. After all, I was the ship's sailing master. Stradling would need me to pilot the ship back home. So I remained on the beach, watching, waiting. The day drew on and a cool wind blew out of the sea, but alas, the ship never returned.

As night fell, I took shelter in the trees, but could not sleep. I was terrified of the dreadful howling of the seals that gathered in their thousands along the shoreline. My fears multiplied in the darkness. I had heard stories about savages who lived on islands like this, and what about the beasts of the forest? I kept my **musket** by my side all night. I even fired it at one point, as the seals seemed to be closing in on me. But this only stopped their moaning for a short time.

The following morning found me back on the beach surrounded by my few possessions and supplies. I flung open my sea chest and took stock of what I had:

- some clothes and bedding
- gunpowder and bullets
- hatchet
- knife
- spyglass
- cooking pot
- navigation instruments and charts
- Bible and prayer book
- three days' worth of food, including salted beef and cheese.

Castaway

Later, I explored the beach, without venturing inland. I came upon a hut that had been hastily built, made out of sailcloth and bits of wood. One of the previous visitors to the island must have set it up. I moved my trunk into it then gazed out at my new home. The bay was wide and flanked by some of the island's huge sea-cliffs. The land behind it rose steeply towards a ridge of mountains.

I waited and watched. Even if my own ship never came back, I still hoped that another one – perhaps the *St George* – would.

But what if it was not a friendly ship? After thinking about it for a while, I decided that if a French ship came in then I would surrender to them. I would be throwing myself on their mercy, but there was a fair chance I would live. I would never surrender to the Spanish though, for I knew they would spare no stranger. Feeling helpless, miserable, and full of remorse, I slumped on the beach with my head in my hands.

There I remained while I worked my way through my supplies. I lamented my lack of salt. What little meat I had soon ran out, so I wandered along the shore searching for something else. I found crabs and clams in the shallows, and large spiny lobsters and sea turtles.

I ate some of the seafood but it gave me a terrible stomach upset, which knocked me out for days on end. I became weak and feverish and would have gladly died at this point, such was my misery. But somehow ... I did not.

Instead, I rose from my makeshift bed and built a fire. I boiled up some water, and picked some herbs from the banks of a stream to flavour it. I was delighted to discover mint among the herbs, since I knew this was considered good for ailments of the gut. As I recovered, my despair gave way to a kind of acceptance. I rolled up my sleeves and set about the business of survival.

Castaway

The first thing I needed to do was find better shelter away from the beach, away from the wind and rain and the dreadful howling of the seals which plagued my sleep. I began exploring the island. On the first day, I climbed several hundred feet[3] up a steep mountain pass, through forests dense with giant ferns and tiny red hummingbirds.

At the top of the pass the view opened out. From here I could see much of the island, my new home, as well as the gleaming blue ocean around it. From here, I could scan the horizon for ships. I constructed a beacon out of dry grass and wood. If I spotted any friendly ships, then I would set it ablaze to make my presence known.

In time, I would make this same trek almost every day. I came to know this spot as my lookout.

[3] Selkirk climbed about 550 metres.

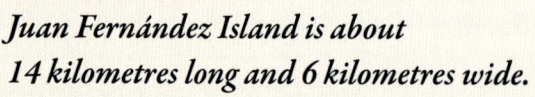

Juan Fernández Island is about 14 kilometres long and 6 kilometres wide.

Juan Fernández Island

The Great Bay, where Selkirk landed, offered ships some protection from the fury of the Pacific storms. The giant cliffs meant there weren't many other places for a ship to anchor. The island was dominated by a spine of volcanic mountains. Between the mountains were lush gorges and valleys filled with waterfalls and fern forests. There were also grasslands, fringed by sandalwood trees and cabbage palms.

The climate was pleasant: the winters were mild and the summers were warm but not too hot. The ocean made the climate changeable too. The sea air blew in, condensed as it rose over the mountains and then fell as rain. This gave rise to the island's many torrents and streams. Herbs, turnips and wild oats grew on the streams' banks.

Thanks to the abundance of food and water, Selkirk had much of what he needed to survive … for now.

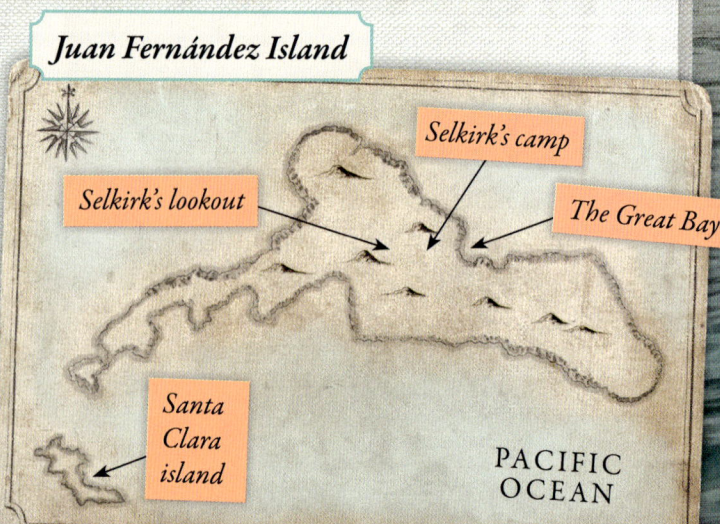

Fur seals and southern elephant seals lounged on the beaches of the island.

Hundreds of kilometres separated the island from the coast of Chile, which lay to the east. To the west there were thousands upon thousands of kilometres of open ocean.

Life often arrived on the island by chance:

- Strong ocean winds brought bees, flies and seeds.

- Other creatures arrived on pieces of driftwood, such as spiders, worms, insect pupae, and even snakes. More had arrived on the soles of long-gone visiting sailors' shoes.

- The occasional ship which had landed in the past had brought cats and rats.

- Many years before, Spanish sailors had introduced goats to ensure they had a supply of meat should they ever have cause to land there.

- Birds were often marooned there too, carried by strong currents or blown in by the winds: swans, puffins, and even the odd penguin.

Selkirk may have been alone, but he wasn't the only castaway.

Castaway

As the days drew into months, I began to make the island a home. One day, while hunting goats on the mountainside high over the bay, I chanced upon an open glade: a shady, sheltered spot, fanned by gentle breezes. A stream ran through it and herbs, parsnips, turnips and cabbages grew nearby. It was perfect. Here I built myself a hut.

Using what tools I had, I fashioned a raised platform out of wood, which I used as a bed, along with a crude chair and table. I dragged my sea chest up from the beach with some difficulty. I lined the walls of the hut with goatskins as protection from the gusting winds.

I also began to build up my stores. I swept the beaches, where ships had landed in the past, seizing upon items that people had thrown away, such as rusty nails, broken barrel hoops and old rope. To my surprise, I began to discover depths of resourcefulness that I never knew I had. I built myself a large firepit out of stones, right in the centre of my camp, which I endeavoured to keep burning day and night. Then I constructed a forge. I used odd bits and pieces of metal to create fish hooks and axe heads. I carved a spade out of wood, hardening its head by slowly and gently charring it over the glimmering embers of my campfire. I made more new tools and used them to make items such as plates and bowls.

Fuelled by my success thus far, I constructed a second, smaller hut on the other side of the stream to act as a larder and kitchen. I found suitable plants to thatch the roofs of both huts.

✽ ✽ ✽

My gunpowder and bullets soon began to run out. This terrified me at first, because it meant that my only way of hunting the goats was to chase after them. They were fast, nimble creatures. It took time to master the skills needed, but I soon became adept at catching them. I gained greater home comforts by carving knives and forks out of the goats' horns.

While I was much happier to be away from the beach and the constant moaning of the seals and sea lions, I soon discovered that I had a different problem.

Castaway

Juan Fernández Island swarmed with countless rats. Their ancestors must have jumped from ships such as my own and those vermin had bred and multiplied many times over. Rats were a constant nuisance to me in my new camp. Sleep eluded me night after night as I waited for them to creep towards me in the dark. Then I could feel them gnawing at me, nibbling through my clothing. My solution was to turn to the island's population of **feral** cats.

I began by befriending kittens, offering them food. Having tamed the creatures, I surrounded myself with them. I slept with them curled up around me. After that, I had no trouble from rats again. My cats drove them away. They also provided me with some much-needed company.

My biggest nightmare was that if something very serious happened to me, no one would be there to help, or even, should I die, to bury my body. That nightmare nearly came true one day.

I was pursuing a goat in the woods. The creature dived into some bushes, and I followed after it, grabbing it round the body. Suddenly, the ground fell away. The bushes had hidden a precipice, jutting over a steep drop. I tumbled to the bottom. My head cracked against a rock, and I passed out.

When I woke, hours might have gone by, but it might also have been days. I was suffering from severe pain and the goat was lying underneath me. The poor animal had taken the brunt of the fall. In fact, it had saved my life. I had that to be thankful for at least.

✱ ✱ ✱

Castaway

I could barely move. I lay there overnight with the cold seeping into my bones, hoping my strength might return, but it didn't. In the morning, I started to crawl. I had no idea how long it would take me to get back to my camp, which was about a mile distant, but I had no option. It was either crawl or surely die in this dark, damp hollow. I dragged myself through the forest by my fingertips, an agonizingly slow and painful experience. By the time I reached home my fire had long since gone out. I dragged my battered, scratched limbs into bed and fell asleep. I counted ten days and nights before I could move again.

When finally I stumbled out of my hut I was very weak indeed. Even so, I was overwhelmed with relief; I was still alive, and had been spared the fate of my nightmares. The first thing I did was to re-light my fire, rubbing sticks together in **tinder**, resolving never to let it die again. Then I picked up my Bible and began to read.

***

As the long months drew on, I slowly began to accept my life of solitude. I still made my daily trek up to my lookout. There I sat, day after day, scanning the horizon, seeing nothing: no sails, no wake in the distance, not even a tiny dot that might be construed as a ship. Nothing but blue ocean.

And yet, there was something strangely comforting and peaceful about this spot. The only sound to be heard was the call of a distant bird, or the wind rustling through the grass. I began to realize what solitude, real solitude, was actually like – going through every day for months, even years on end, without meeting or speaking to a single soul; knowing that there wasn't a single human being within four hundred miles. I was as alone as it was possible to be.

Castaway

By now, my beard and hair had grown long. My skin was sunburned and weathered. My clothes had fallen apart, so I set about making myself new ones – a brand-new outfit appropriate for my new station as King of the Island. I fashioned it out of goatskins, sewing them together using an old nail as a needle and thread unwound from one of my socks. When my shoes wore out I didn't bother to make new ones, finding it easier to go barefoot. My feet became rough and calloused, as hard and impenetrable as leather. I could leap across boulders, scale cliffs. I became more nimble and agile even than the goats I pursued. I ceased being frightened of savages and the beasts of the forest. I even learned how to hunt the giant sea lions who battled each other in the surf. Their fat became my cooking oil and their fur replaced my worn-out bedding.

I tried to keep track of time, carving a notch in a tree every day, but some days I forgot, or was too busy, so I soon lost track. The longer I lived on the island, the easier survival became. In fact I would go so far as to say I had become comfortable. I was an expert on the island's plants, animals and freshwater springs. Every once in a while, I would climb to a point high in the mountains, where tiny black plums studded the trees, and I would carry them home and make jam out of them. I had a more varied and plentiful diet than any I'd experienced on board ship. One day I would eat goat broth with cabbage, another it would be roast fish, and another seal with turnips, or lobster.

Life on the island may have been lonely, but it was also enriching. I found quiet depths within my soul – a soul which once had been angry and troubled, but was no longer. Perhaps it was due to the peace and tranquillity, or to reading every day. Or perhaps it was just the lack of other people to come into conflict with.

Stradling's Fate

Selkirk was right about the *Cinque Ports*. As he predicted, shipworms ate through the bottom of the ship. About a month after abandoning Selkirk, the *Cinque Ports* sank off the island of Malpelo, near the Peruvian coast (now in Colombia).

Most of the crew perished. The survivors, including Captain Stradling, threw themselves on the Spaniards' mercy. They were fortunate their captors didn't execute them. Instead they were marched overland to the Peruvian city of Lima, where they were imprisoned in a dank jail. Conditions were harsh and their numbers dwindled still further.

Stradling spent four years rotting in his Peruvian prison, although he attempted to escape twice. It was many years before he made it home to Britain, a broken and penniless man.

Stradling's escape

- finally makes it home to Britain
- taken to France
- Cinque Ports *sinks*
- escape to Panama
- Lima jail

Dampier's Fate

The *St George*, the *Cinque Ports*'s sister ship which was captained by William Dampier, fared little better after it parted ways with the *Cinque Ports*. It too was in a parlous state, with timbers so badly chewed by shipworms they were said to be as thin as a sixpence.[4]

Dampier did, however, manage to track down the fabled Manila galleon. The ship's name was *Rosario*. It was well-defended and Dampier knew his ship was hopelessly out-gunned, but the crew were desperate for a prize, so they took the Spanish ship on.

They planned a stealth attack, but Dampier got cold feet and called it off. To the crew's dismay, the big prize escaped. After all the risks they had taken and hardships they had suffered, the men were furious. They blamed their captain, and, in the face of mutiny, Dampier decided they would cut their losses and head home.

The *St George* sailed west across the Pacific but soon had to be abandoned due to its lack of seaworthiness. What remained of the crew hijacked another ship to take them the rest of the way home.

It had been a disastrous expedition for both the *Cinque Ports* and the *St George*. Only a few of the crew made it home. In some ways, though he did not know it at the time, Selkirk was the lucky one.

[4] An old coin

Castaway

As the months drew into years, I became attuned to the rhythm of island life and the turn of its seasons. I lived a plain and natural existence. Despite the hardship and loneliness, I found great peace in it.

My daily routine involved visiting my lookout, fishing, hunting, tending my fire and cooking. I often thought about the things that I had found indispensable in my old life: things such as salt, proper clothes and shoes. I no longer missed such things. They were simply unnecessary in my new world.

In time, I extended the camp further, building a large pen for the goats. I churned their milk and made cheese with it. I built a sturdy raft out of the trunks of palm trees, tied together with strips of bark, and made a wooden paddle. On calm days, I would often set out around the coastline on my raft so as to explore more of my island home. I also made a fishing rod and used goat **sinews** for the fishing line. My fear of starvation had long since gone.

The rest of the time I spent at rest back at my shaded camp, reading. My sleep was untroubled; I no longer suffered nightmares. I fashioned a small flute, on which I played simple tunes. On clear nights, when the stars were out, I would bring out my old navigational instruments and peer up at the stars, the distant constellations and planets.

From time to time I still felt lonely, but my contentment with my fate grew. My old shipboard life and my native Scotland became a distant dream. At night, bathed in the light from my fire, I sang and danced with only my cats for company. In fact, I never danced with a lighter heart or greater spirit than I did to the sound of my own voice with the dumb animals.[5]

The island provided for all my necessities: food, water, shelter. Beyond that, the more time I spent alone, the more I began to see the island as my own. With my goatskin clothes and cap, and bare feet, I felt I was truly the monarch of all I surveyed.

✽ ✽ ✽

---

[5] 'Dumb animals' is an old phrase which refers to the fact that animals cannot speak.

Castaway

One morning, my solitude was finally broken – but in the worst possible way. I woke to find that a ship had dropped anchor in the Great Bay, flying the colours of Spain.

Smaller boats – **yawls** and **pinnaces** – were landing on the beach, and they were full of armed men. Watching from the scrub behind the beach, I knew it meant trouble. My instinct for survival rose within me and I fled. Unfortunately, a keen-eyed sailor must have spotted me, for the Spaniards gave chase. I heard their yells and cries behind me. 'Perro!' they shouted (meaning 'dog'). They fired their muskets and a musket ball whizzed close past my ear.

Castaway

The Spaniards were numerous, but none of them knew the island like I did. I weaved through the dense bushes and climbed through a gully, heading straight for the thick woods on the eastern side of the island. There, I climbed a tree, where I concealed myself for days while the Spaniards trawled the bush hunting for me. Then, just as suddenly as they'd arrived, their ship **weighed anchor** and left.

I returned to my camp to find it burned to the ground. All my tame goats were dead. These interlopers had destroyed almost everything, even my Bible and navigational instruments.

Strangely, I was untroubled by all this. The old Alexander Selkirk would have ranted and raved, and probably made the wreckage even worse. But I was not the hot-headed man I had been before. Instead, I calmly set to work, building a new firepit and forge, chopping wood, hammering and cutting. Within a short space of time I had rebuilt my huts, and this time I made some improvements, such as a new bed. I scoured the beach where the Spaniards had made their camp, for their litter was my bounty: coins, empty bottles, rusty metal, pieces of sailcloth, bits of chain and rope. Everything could be useful.

All things considered, by the end of this unfortunate episode my living conditions were just as good, if not better, than they were before.

imagine!

How might the bottles, metal, cloth, chain and rope have been useful to Selkirk? What could he have made with them?

The *Duke* and *Dutchess*

Captain Dampier's first expedition with the *St George* might have failed disastrously, but he wasn't the kind of man to be defeated. After he finally made his way back to England in 1707, he had no trouble raising money for a new expedition. Men's eyes glimmered as he told them about all the Spanish gold there for the taking in the South Seas, and about the riches of the Manila galleon. He blamed the disasters of the first expedition on bad luck, an ill-disciplined crew and, of course, worms eating through the bottom of the ships.

However, this time Dampier would not be in charge of the expedition. His official title was 'South Seas pilot', and his role was to navigate the ships once they got to the Pacific. Instead, a Bristol man called Woodes Rogers was appointed. Rogers would also be captain of one of the ships.

Rogers was about 30 years old, tall and confident and from a wealthy family. He was respectful of his crew, and they respected him too. He was fair, but also a stiff disciplinarian.

Captain Dampier
now South Seas pilot

Captain Woodes Rogers
captain of the *Duke*

The investors paid for two **frigates** to be fitted out. This time the hulls were specially constructed to protect against the dreaded shipworms. The first ship, called the *Duke*, was 80 feet[6] long, 320 tonnes and had a crew of 117. The second ship, called the *Dutchess*, was slightly smaller at 260 tonnes and had a crew of 108.

The ships left Bristol on 2nd August 1708, heading south – almost five years after the *Cinque Ports* and the *St George* had set out on the same voyage.

Months later, as the ships rounded Cape Horn, the weather was cold and stormy. The crew were hungry and exhausted, and many were suffering from scurvy. They urgently needed a safe harbour where they could resupply, and the nearest place was Juan Fernández.

Captain Rogers's ship's log

1st February 1709, Juan Fernández island
We moored some four leagues off the island of Juan Fernández. About two in the afternoon, some of the crew set off in the pinnace, aiming for the great middle bay. It took them some hours to reach land.

[6] about 24.5 metres

Castaway

It was January 1709 when my solitude came to an end. I was cooking outside my hut when I spotted a lone sail on the horizon. For a moment time stood still as I watched the sail grow ever closer. Then a second ship appeared. I saw no Spanish or French colours so I knew they must be English ships. Something in my head convinced me that it was the *Cinque Ports* and the *St George*, returning to the island. The ships anchored some distance outside the Great Bay. I watched as a small boat full of men cast off from one of the ships, then rowed towards shore.

Yet even now I hesitated to make myself known. I realized that a part of me loved this island. My island. I loved my simple and uncomplicated life there. And I did not want to leave it. Part of me, perhaps, hoped the ships would pass on, leaving me once again in my solitude. I hated the idea of meeting Stradling again – the man who'd marooned me here. I determined that if Stradling was with them I would refuse to get on board. Even after four years alone, I would rather have died on the island than get on a ship with that man again.

Nevertheless, I knew I could not let the chance of rescue pass me by. I dragged a burning log to the shore and built up a huge bonfire. I stood at the water's edge and waited to welcome the men in the boat.

imagine!
If you were Selkirk, would you have signalled to the ship, not knowing for sure if it was friendly?

Castaway

Captain Rogers's ship's log

1st February 1709, Juan Fernández island
As it got dark, as our boat was halfway to the island, we saw a light ashore. We believed it to be an enemy signal, perhaps from a ship, therefore we signalled our boat to return. We then sailed around the south of the island, in order to deceive any enemies that might have been watching. We intended to land on the island with the first southerly wind, which Captain Dampier said blows nearly all the time, the next morning.

Castaway

The Duke and Dutchess sailing away from the fire

The Great Bay

Juan Fernández Island

Just as rescue seemed so close, the boat suddenly turned round and rowed back to the ship. My doubts melted away. Now I knew I wanted to be rescued. I despaired as I watched the ships sailing off towards the south of the island. I could hardly believe that they'd come so close, only to turn around and leave. Only now did I realize that my bonfire might not have been seen as a welcome.

Panicking, I climbed up to my lookout. I remained there until dawn, scanning the seas, but I could see nothing of the ships. My heart sank. I had lost my chance of rescue.

* * *

Later that morning, I returned to the beach, dejected and sad. I immediately spotted a rowing boat approaching the shoreline. I did not even have a second thought, but ran towards them, yelling and waving a stick with a white rag attached.

As the men turned to face me, they raised their guns. Were they going to shoot me?

One way or the other, my four-and-a-half-year ordeal was at an end.

III. THE JOURNEY HOME, 1709

Aboard

Sitting outside the bay on the *Duke*, Rogers was beginning to get worried, as the men had been gone for some time. Meanwhile on the beach, the men assured Selkirk that there was no one called Stradling on the ship. Only then did he agree to come aboard with them. When the boat finally returned to the *Duke*, Rogers was astonished by what he saw.

> Rogers commented that the crew brought back 'an abundance of crawfish and a man cloth'd in goat skins, who looked wilder than the first owners of them.'

Selkirk climbed aboard, barefoot and hardly able to speak. As the deck rose and fell on the sea swell, he stumbled and gripped the handrail. He was unused to a ship's movement after so long on land.

The crew stared at this strange curiosity of a man. Rogers began asking him questions. Fortunately, there were some familiar faces from the previous expedition. Not least there was Dampier himself, who confirmed Selkirk's identity. They crowded around him and offered him food, but he found it revolting: he wasn't used to the salt.

Selkirk began to tell them his story. He told them everything: about his camp, his lookout spot, his cats and goats, and even about the small black plums he picked from high up on the mountainside. He told them about the day the Spaniards came and the day he nearly died falling off a cliff.

No one could quite believe he'd survived so long in such a place. They shaved his beard and trimmed his hair. They provided new clothes and shoes. It took him a while to get used to wearing shoes again as they made his feet swell up.

Woodes Rogers's diary

The *Duke*'s captain was fascinated by Selkirk's story and wrote down a detailed account of it in his diary. He mischievously referred to Selkirk as the 'Governor of Juan Fernández'. He was impressed by Selkirk's apparent peace of mind.

> Rogers put Selkirk's survival down to his 'plain and temperate way of living – fresh air, daily exercise, plenty of fresh fruits and vegetables.'

Selkirk took the officers ashore and showed them his camp. He also showed off his goat-hunting prowess.

Many of the crew were suffering from scurvy. They were carried ashore, where a makeshift hospital was set up on the beach, with tents made out of old sails. Meanwhile, the ships were repaired, and work parties cut wood and filled water casks.

Selkirk spent that time hunting and catching food. He showed the crew the best spots for fishing. He also pointed out where to find herbs and greens. He tended the sick, cooking up goat broth with cabbages and turnips. Most of the ill were soon up and about.

It was a little after three in the afternoon on 13th February 1709 when the ship departed Juan Fernández. Rogers learned from Dampier that Selkirk was a veteran seaman and a skilled navigator, so Rogers appointed Selkirk second mate on the *Duke*. Selkirk's new duties kept him busy but he must have watched from the **stern** as the island, *his* island, slid below the horizon behind him. The Great Bay, the mountains and cliffs that he'd spent so many years with, faded into his past.

He'd left his camp behind, his home-made tools and his goats, along with the dying embers of his fire.

imagine!
How would it feel to return to normal life after four years as a castaway?

He didn't have time to dwell on it, though. Nor could he think of home. Not yet. As second mate on the *Duke* he had to prepare for action. The crew had set their sights on booty. The ships were heading up the west coast of South America, where they hoped to attack merchant ships, raid towns and seek out the Manila galleon.

Back to a Life at Sea

Over the next few weeks, Selkirk returned to his life as a privateer with enthusiasm. He seemed to relish company and action again. The *Duke* and *Dutchess* captured several small merchant ships and Selkirk was made ship's master of one of them, which they called *Increase*.

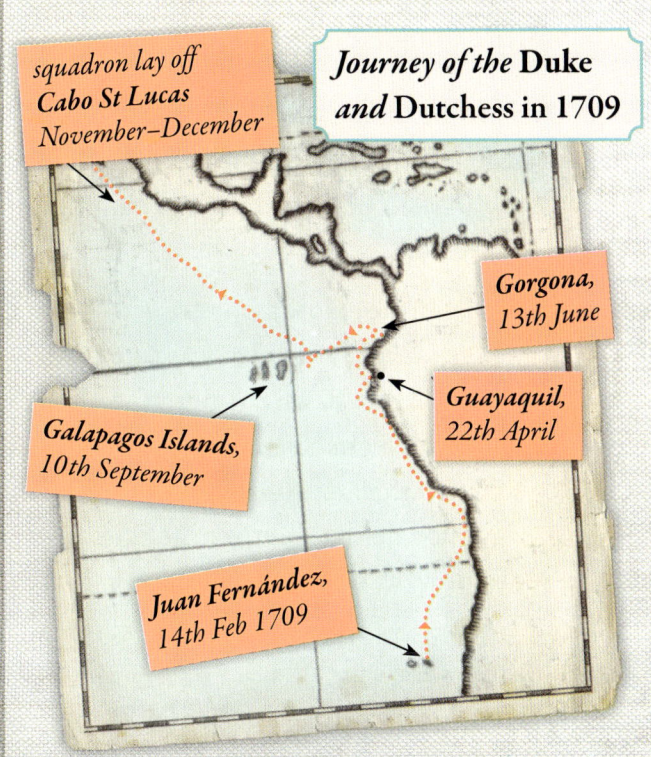

squadron lay off **Cabo St Lucas** November–December

Journey of the* Duke *and* Dutchess *in 1709

Gorgona, 13th June

Guayaquil, 22th April

Galapagos Islands, 10th September

Juan Fernández, 14th Feb 1709

Next, they landed in Ecuador and attacked the town of Guayaquil. They fought a battle with the town's defenders, before looting and burning many buildings. Eventually they were paid by the town to leave.

As the privateers trooped back to their ships, they reckoned it had been a decent haul. But for the expedition to be a success they needed a much greater treasure: they still needed the Manila galleon.

Back at sea, they took station along the galleon's most likely route, but to no avail. The months drew on, their supplies dwindled and as before, the crew became mutinous. By December 1709 they were about to give up and head home, but then the crew saw something on the horizon that brought with it a flicker of hope.

Rogers recorded the moment in his diary: 'To our great and joyful surprise, about 9 o'clock the man on the masthead cried out he saw a sail bearing west, about seven leagues away.'

Dampier judged it to be a frigate of 400 tonnes and declared that it could only be the Manila galleon they'd dreamt of seizing all these long months. The privateer fleet immediately gave chase. This was a different treasure galleon from the one Dampier had fought many years before. It was newer, stronger and better defended. Her name was *Nuestra Señora de la Encarnación y Desengaño* (*Our Lady of Incarnation and Disappointment*) and Dampier estimated the ship and its cargo to be worth a million pounds.

The ship was a long way from being theirs for the taking, though. It bristled with heavy cannons and was manned by nearly 200 crewmen. How were they to take such a ship? They would need to use all their guile and determination. They would have to outwit her.

All day they closed on the *Desengaño*. Their plan was to board her at dawn the next morning. The Spanish must have known this, for their sailors hung gunpowder barrels over the sides to prevent boarding.

At first light, Captain Rogers gathered his crew around him on the deck and gave a rousing speech. Mugs of hot chocolate were dished out, and the men readied themselves for the attack.

Captain Rogers's ship's log

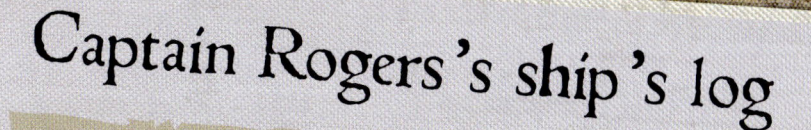

22nd December 1709, high seas off California

It was the enemy who opened fire on us first, blasting cannon shot over our heads. The Dutchess had little wind to come up and help. As we closed on the ship over the course of the next few hours, the enemy fired at us using the small cannons on their stern. We fired back, aiming for their exposed rudder. We pulled alongside and then fired the cannons at her again, while the crew fired their pistols and muskets all at once, and sharpshooters picked off the Spanish gunners. We then drove our ship along the big ship's side. This was enough for the enemy, who surrendered.

Treasure at last!

Selkirk and his fellow crewmen boarded the surrendered ship. They'd captured the fabled treasure galleon and with only light casualties. The crew could hardly believe their luck. At last they had the treasure they needed. They could go home.

The treasures of the Manila galleon

- gold dust
- gold plate
- gold coins
- silver plates
- necklaces
- pearls
- rubies and diamonds
- gold and jade statues
- spices
- **musk**
- textiles
- sets of rare china (including a set intended for the Spanish Queen)
- silks, fans, stockings, gowns, oil paintings and many other precious and valuable commodities.

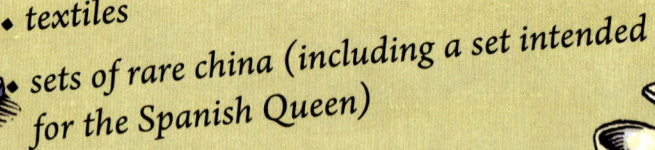

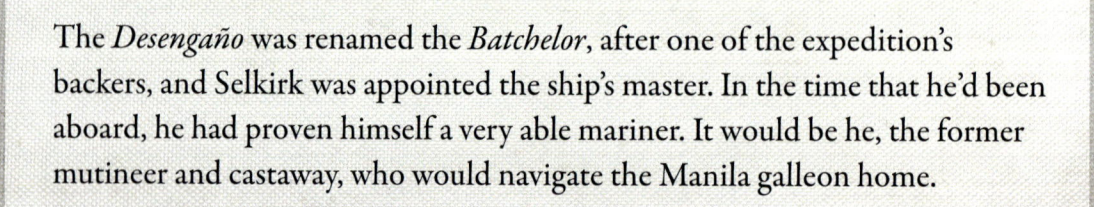

The *Desengaño* was renamed the *Batchelor*, after one of the expedition's backers, and Selkirk was appointed the ship's master. In the time that he'd been aboard, he had proven himself a very able mariner. It would be he, the former mutineer and castaway, who would navigate the Manila galleon home.

Home

It took nearly two years to travel the 30 000 kilometres west back to England, via Guam, Batavia (now Jakarta) and Cape Town. On the way, the crew had to face further sea battles, starvation, disease and even attacks by ravenous sharks. But at 11am on 14th October 1711, the voyage finally came to an end.

When Selkirk stepped on to the dry land alongside the Thames at Erith, he was wearing a brand-new outfit, complete with a waistcoat made of swanskin, a blue linen shirt and shoes with scarlet laces. He looked very different from the man who'd climbed aboard at Juan Fernández.

He'd been away eight years, circumnavigated the globe and survived alone for half of that time on an uninhabited island. He was a man who had a story to tell, but would anyone want to hear it?

Selkirk brought his sea chest all the way home with him.

imagine!
What would you want to ask Selkirk when he finally returned home?

Telling Selkirk's story

Two of the men from the expedition kept diaries. The first, of course, was Captain Woodes Rogers and the other was Edward Cooke, who had been one of the senior officers.

On their return, both men published accounts of their voyage. Cooke's book came out first in 1712. He didn't think anyone would be very interested in Selkirk's story, so he gave it only passing attention, devoting the rest to describing the great storms, the sea battles, the booty and the various arguments between the crew.

> February 2. In the Morning ... we row'd and tow'd into the great Bay, and came to an Anchor in 50 Fathom[7] Water ... The *Duke's* Boat went ashore, and found one Alexander Selkirk ... He was cloath'd in a Goat's Skin jacket, Breeches, and Cap, sew'd together with Thongs of the same.

Extract from Cooke's book

But readers wanted to know more about the castaway Cooke had briefly mentioned. There was an almost instant fascination with the story of a man marooned on a remote island for many years, surviving on very little except his own wits. Captain Rogers's book gave them much more of the story and, to Selkirk's great surprise, he became something of a celebrity.

Cover of Rogers's book

[7] A fathom is a unit of length, used to measure the depth of water. 50 fathoms is about 90 metres.

Life back on land

Selkirk walked away from the expedition a wealthy man, with £800 – a huge sum, given most seaman were lucky to earn £1 a month. Along with this he also received:
- four gold rings
- a silver box
- a gold-headed cane
- a pair of gold candlesticks
- a sword with a silver hilt.

> When interviwed by Richard Steele, Selkirk said, 'I am now worth eight hundred pounds, but I shall never be so happy as when I was not worth a farthing.'

For a while Selkirk played the part of a minor celebrity, accepting invitations to a lot of parties across London, but it was not the life for him.

For all the joys and comforts of civilization, he began to miss his life on the island terribly. His cats and goats, the view from his lookout, even the moaning of the sea lions on the beach.

Apparently there was talk of another expedition, and Selkirk was keen to be a part of it. He hung around the port of Bristol waiting for it to come together, but it never did. Then the Treaties of Utrecht were signed with Spain which brought the war, and the era of privateers in the South Seas, to an end.

As the months passed, Selkirk became restless and unhappy, falling into his old bad habits of getting into fights. When he was charged with assaulting another sailor, he didn't wait around for the trial. He fled Bristol and headed home to Largo in Scotland.

Largo

It was 1714 when Selkirk returned to Scotland. His parents, who'd thought him dead, wept with joy. He wore gold-laced clothes, which instantly set him apart in his poor fishing village. He looked every bit the successful man.

But Selkirk found it hard to adjust to being home again. He'd lived a life of adventure, while in Largo things went on much the same as they had before. He found the humdrum conversation around the dining table a real strain. His parents talked of church gossip and sheep grazing. Their outlook seemed very narrow compared to his own.

Selkirk soon became sad and listless. He built a kind of cave in a crag behind his father's house. He would go there alone and sit and watch the sea. His parents were worried by his behaviour. They trudged up the hill to speak to him, only to find him in tears. 'Oh, my beloved island,' he cried. 'I wish I'd never left thee.'

Selkirk didn't stay at home for long. He got into another fight and then left, this time for good. He headed back to London. He later married and joined the Royal Navy. He became part of the crew on the HMS *Enterprise*, followed by HMS *Weymouth*.

In 1721, disease swept through the crew of the HMS *Weymouth*. After four years as a sailor again, Alexander Selkirk died at sea in December 1721.

The Real Robinson Crusoe

A famous writer called Daniel Defoe read about Selkirk's story and it inspired him to write a **novel**. That novel was *Robinson Crusoe*, one of the first novels written in the English language. It was published in 1719 and became an instant success. There are many differences between Selkirk's story and that of Robinson Crusoe, the main character in Defoe's novel:

	Alexander Selkirk	Robinson Crusoe
Island location	South Seas	Caribbean
How did he get there?	marooned	shipwrecked
What supplies did he have?	basic items including cooking pot and musket	wealth of supplies from his ship – including a goatskin umbrella!
What was his camp like?	two huts, a forge and a fire-pit	two houses with defensive walls, a fine garden and an orchard
Who else was there with him?	no one else set foot on the island, except the Spaniards who tried to shoot Selkirk	a man he called Friday who lived on the island – at the end of the story Friday went with Crusoe to England

But the main difference between Crusoe's story and Selkirk's – and the one that makes Selkirk's story more interesting – is that Selkirk's is all true, whereas Crusoe's is all fiction.

Juan Fernández Island was renamed Robinson Crusoe Island in the 1960s. The Chilean government wanted to use Selkirk's story to attract tourists. Another island in the **archipelago** was renamed after Selkirk himself. However, this island is about 160 kilometres to the west and, as far as we can tell, Selkirk never set foot on it.

Engraving of Robinson Crusoe from Defoe's book

Castaway

Throughout the whole four and a half years he was marooned, Selkirk longed for rescue. The thought of it kept him going and drove him to climb up to his lookout, day after day, to scan the seas. Yet there was something about his life there that held him, enriched him. It made him a better man. The island spoke to him and made him a part of it. The ravines and the jagged mountain peaks, the giant ferns and tiny red hummingbirds, the sound of waves lapping on the shore, and the squally winds blowing off the sea. The rhythm of the seasons coming and going. All of it echoed with the natural grace that touched a simple man's soul.

To this day, visitors climb the steep pass to gaze over Selkirk's lookout. A bronze plaque marks the spot where the castaway kept his long, lonely vigil. Selkirk's body was buried at sea, but it would be comforting to think that his soul rests here, looking out over the island he once called his own.

The End

Note on Sources

William Funnell, *A Voyage Round the World* (1707)

Edward Cooke, *A Voyage to the South Sea and Round the World* (1712)

Woodes Rogers, *A Cruising Voyage Round the World* (1712)

Richard Steele, *The Englishman* [26] (1–3 December 1713)

John Howell, *The Life and Adventures of Alexander Selkirk* (1829)

The interview notes, diaries and ship's logs in this book are fictional constructions adapted from and based on real sources and events.

Maps showing routes and journeys are approximations based on available evidence.

Quotations are adapted in places for clarity.

Glossary

archipelago (*say* ark-i-pel-ago): a group of islands
booty: anything valuable that is taken from a captured ship
castaway: someone who has been abandoned or shipwrecked
elders: older or senior members of a community
farthing: an old coin that was worth a quarter of a penny
feral: something that has gone wild
frigates: medium-sized warships
galleon: a large ship with three or more masts, used as a warship or trading ship
hull: the main body of a ship
journal: a kind of newspaper
lieutenant: (*say* lef-tenant) a naval officer, junior to the captain
man-of-war: a kind of warship
marooned: abandoned on an isolated shore
munitions: ammunition and guns
musk: a strong-smelling substance used in perfumes
musket: a kind of long-barrelled gun
mutinies: rebellions on ships, where the crew turn against the captain
mutinous: rebellious
novel: a story written in prose that is long enough to be a book
pinnaces: ships' small boats, usually with oars, used to transport things or people between the ships and the shore, or to another ship (similar to yawls)
sea chest: a large wooden box which sailors used to store their belongings in
ship's master: the crew member responsible mainly for navigating the vessel
shipworms: wormlike molluscs that bore into wood
sinews: the strong tissues linking muscles to bones
stern: the rear end of the ship
tinder: any dry substance that catches fire easily – usually small twigs
weevils: a kind of beetle
weighed anchor: hauled up the anchor in order to be ready to sail
yawls: ships' small boats, usually with four or six oars (similar to pinnaces)

Index

Articles of Agreement 8
Acapulco galleon .... (see Manila galleon)
Asunción (Spanish ship) 17, 18
Cape Horn 4, 12, 15, 16, 36
careening 19
Chile 4, 25, 51
Cinque Ports (ship) 6–9, 14, 16–20, 30–31, 36
Cooke, Edward 48, 53
Dampier, William 7, 15, 17–18, 31, 35, 38, 40, 42, 44
Defoe, Daniel 51
Desengaño (Spanish treasure ship) 44, 46
Duke (frigate) 4, 15, 35–36, 39, 40, 42, 43
Dutchess (frigate) 4, 35–36, 39, 43, 45
Englishman, The (journal) 5, 53
Guayaquil, Ecuador 43
Juan Fernández (island) 4–5, 7, 19, 24–25, 27, 36, 38–39, 41–42, 43, 51
Largo, Fife, Scotland 6, 49, 50
letter of marque 7–8
Manila galleon .... (see also *Rosario* and *Desengaño*) 15, 18, 31, 35, 42–44, 46
navigation 12–13, 21, 32, 34
Pickering, Captain Charles 6–7, 16
privateers 7–9, 11, 14–15, 17, 43–44, 49
prize ships 15, 17, 31, 45
Robinson Crusoe 51
Rogers, Captain Woodes 35–36, 38, 40–45, 48, 53
Rosario (Spanish treasure ship) 31
St George (ship) 6–7, 16–18, 31, 35
scurvy 16, 36, 41
sea lions 26, 29, 49
Selkirk's lookouts 23, 24, 28, 32, 39, 41, 49, 52
shipworms 19, 30–31, 35–36
Steele, Richard 5, 21, 49, 53
Stradling, Thomas 16–18, 20–21, 30, 37, 40
War of the Spanish Succession 9

About the Author

I'm quite a lucky person because I've always known what I wanted to do with my life, which is to write. I began writing at around 8 years old, and have been writing ever since. I have written books, plays and also for the TV.

As an adventure, Selkirk's story has everything – danger and unexplored seas, pirates, sea battles, Spanish treasure galleons. It's a story of survival, of a man falling back on his own resources to stay alive.

Yet for me there's something else. In his time on the island Selkirk knew loneliness, isolation and hardship. But he also knew contentment and he knew freedom. True freedom. The freedom to create a world to call his own.

Greg Foot, Series Editor

I've loved science ever since the day I took my papier mâché volcano into school. I filled it with far too much baking powder, vinegar and red food colouring, and WHOOSH! I covered the classroom ceiling in red goo. Now I've got the best job in the world: I present TV shows for the BBC, answer kids' science questions on YouTube and tell science stories on stage at festivals!

Working on TreeTops inFact has been great fun. There are so many brilliant books, and guess what … they're all packed full of awesome facts! What's your favourite?